Mission Impossible

A comedy
David Muncaster

New Theatre Publications - London
www.plays4theatre.com

The edition published in 2013

New Theatre Publications

2 Hereford Close | Warrington | Cheshire | WA1 4HR | 01925 485605

www.plays4theatre.com   email: info@plays4theatre.com

New Theatre Publications is the trading name of the publishing house that is owned by members of the Playwrights' Co-operative. This innovative project was launched on the 1st October 1997 by writers Paul Beard and Ian Hornby with the aim of encouraging the writing and promotion of the very best in New Theatre by Professional and Amateur writers for the Professional and Amateur Theatre at home and abroad.

ISBN 9 781 840 94933 9

Characters
Angela - *age 20 – 50, very smartly dressed. Cheesy cheerful*
Tim - *age20 – 50, untidy business clothes. A bit of a joker*
Brian - *age 20 – 50, untidy business clothes. Disinterested*
Jacquie - *age 30 – 50, cheap suit. Self important*
Caroline - *age 20 – 40, standard business clothes. A little unstable*

Copyright Information

Video-Recording of Amateur Productions

Performing Licence Applications

A performing licence for these plays will be issued by "New Theatre Publications" subject to the following conditions.

Conditions

1. That the performance fee is paid in full on the date of application for a licence.

2. That the name of the author(s) is/are clearly shown in any programme or publicity material.

3. That the author(s) is/are entitled to receive two complimentary tickets to see his/her/their work in performance if they so wish.

4. That a copy of the play is purchased from New Theatre Publications for each named speaking part and a minimum of three copies purchased for backstage use.

5. That a copy of any review be forwarded to New Theatre Publications.

6. That the New Theatre Publications logo is clearly shown on any publicity material. This is available on our website.

Fees

Details of script prices and fees payable for each performance or public reading can be obtained by telephone to (+44) 01925 485605 or to the address below.

Alternatively, latest prices can be obtained from our website www.plays4theatre.com where credit/debit cards can be used for payment.

To apply for a performing licence for any play please write to New Theatre Publications 2 Hereford Close, Warrington, Cheshire WA1 4HR or email info@plays4theatre.com with the following details:-

1. Name and address of theatre company.

2. Details of venue including seating capacity.

3. Dates of proposed performance or public reading.

4. Contact telephone number for Author's complimentary tickets.

Or apply directly via our website at www.plays4theatre.com

Mission Impossible
A Comedy in One Act
by David Muncaster

The play is set in a company meeting room. There might be posters of package holiday destinations on the walls. Two men and two women sit at a large table *(or several tables together)* at an angle that allows them to be both facing the audience and facing Angela who stands next to a flip chart. The men and women sit with their own gender. There are no sound effects and lighting should be 'corporate' throughout. Each participant has a booklet in front of them on the table. Angela has several maker pens for her flipchart one sheet of which, toward the back, has the words **New Company Mission Statement Happy Customers, Happy Holidays** boldly printed on it.

A Meeting Room within the head office of a package holiday company. TIM, Brian, Caroline and Jacquie are sitting at a conference table. Angela is standing by a flipchart. All four are wearing business clothes, though the men are rather scruffy. Angela on the other hand is immaculately dressed in a smart suit.

Angela   Well I guess we'll make a start. Thanks for coming today. My name is Angela and I am a consultant brought in by the company to run this little session today. I am very excited to be working for one of the leading package holiday companies in the UK and I just know that we are going to have a great day today. We are going to start off by doing a little introduction exercise, but before we start I want to make it absolutely clear that what is said between these walls stays between these walls. OK? We trust each other and we have confidence in each other, yeah? OK. If you turn over the first page of your booklets, you will see that there are three questions. Name, brief job description, and why you've come today. Now, I don't want you to fill it in for yourself, I want you all to pair up and fill it in for your partner. Understood? *(There is a general groaning.)* Excellent! OK, off you go. *(The others reluctantly talk in muffled tones whilst Angela walks around the table glancing over shoulders. As she does this, the writers cover up what they have written so she cannot read it.)* Just a few words will do, I am not after War and Peace. *(After a few moments Angela returns to her position near the flipchart.)* OK time's up. Tim, *(She smiles at him.)* would you like to start?

Who is your partner today?

Tim This is Brian. He feeds shit to senior management and he's here today because his colleagues have taken out a restraining order on him. *(The others smirk.)*

Angela Well, thank you for making us laugh Tim. Now what does Brian really do?

Tim I haven't the foggiest.

Angela Brian?

Brian I'm a data analyst.

Angela Ah, now that's your job title Brian. That is your 'label' but what do you actually do? *(When saying the word 'label', Angela makes speech mark signs with her fingers.)*

Brian What Tim said.

Angela Would it be fair to say that you provide management with the information they require?

Brian The information they want to hear, yes.

Angela And now, maybe you could tell us about Tim?

Brian *(sighs.)* This is Tim. It is so long since he did any actual work that he can't remember what it feels like and he has come here today because lunch is included.

(Angela looks at Tim who beams back at her. We get a sense that there is going to be tension between the two of them.)

Angela Right! Well I'm sure we've all learnt something *(Pause.)* valuable from that little exercise, so perhaps we will just move on now. We have a lot to get through and I am sure that we will all learn a lot about each other as the day progresses. Now, onto the purpose of today's session…

Jacquie Excuse me.

Angela Yes?

Jacquie We've done ours.

Angela You've done your what?

Jacquie We've done the introduction exercise. Aren't you going to let us read 'em out?

Angela It's just that we are short of time and…

Jacquie If you're short of time you shouldn't 'ave 'ad us do 'em in the first place.

Angela Oh. Well. *(Smile.)* All right then. Um. Please go ahead.

Jacquie This is Caroline. She's just back from an extended break. She used to work in the call centre, but she's not going back there, and she has come today to make a valuable contribution to the debate.

Angela Splendid!

Caroline This is Jacquie with a Q. She works on reception and she too wants to make a valuable contribution to the debate.

Brian Jacquie with a Q?

Tim Quackie!

Brian Ah.

Angela Right, well, thank you ladies. I'm pleased that we have a diverse set of skills in the room, even though there are only four of you. I'm sure we are going to have a very productive day today. Now! Who can tell me what the company mission statement says?

Jacquie The what?

Tim Let nation speak unto nation?

Brian That's the BBC.

Tim Er. The future's bright, the future's orange?

Brian Mobile phones.

Tim You'll never put a better bit of butter on your knife?

Brian You can't get quicker than a quick fit fitter.

Tin A Mars a day helps you work, rest and play.

Brian Go to work on an egg.

Tim A million housewives every day pick up a tin of beans and say…

Tim/Brian *(together)* Beanz meanz Heinz.

Angela Ha, ha, ha! Oh I can see we are going to have fun today. Very creative boys, but what's the real answer? *(Silence.)* No? *(More silence.)* Well I think that demonstrates why we are here today. You can remember all those catchy slogans, but you cannot remember the company mission statement that is written at the top of every piece of official company stationary. And our job today, our mission, *(Pause for laugh that doesn't come.)* is to come up with a new statement that sums up what the company is all about and is both memorable and meaningful. Isn't that exciting?

Jacquie We're here to write a mission statement?

Angela Yes.

Jacquie I thought it were to put things right.

Angela Put things right?

Jacquie Sort the company out.

Angela What did the invite say?

Jacquie Volunteers wanted to talk about what the company is going to do in the future.

Angela Nearly. It said to define what we do.

Jacquie Same thing.

Brian It means 'define' as in figure out what the hell it is that we do, not change what we do.

Tim *(shocked.)* You mean we don't send people on crap holidays? I always thought that was what we did.

Brian Buggered if I know. All I see is numbers.

Angela Yes. I'm sure that if you had read on a bit, you would have found that the purpose of today's workshop did become quite clear. Never mind. We're here now and I'm sure that we will produce great results if we all work on this together. Yes? *(Nothing.)* Right ho. Let's begin! If you turn to the next page in your little booklet, you'll see a list of words. Caroline, which word in that list sums up the purpose of this company as you see it?

Caroline Sorry?

Angela Turn the page Caroline. *(She does.)* Good. Now which word in that list best describes what this company is all about?

Caroline Er...

Angela In your own time.

Caroline It doesn't make any sense.

Angela Pick a word, any word.

Caroline Wig-wam.

Angela What?

Caroline I don't know, you said to say anything.

Angela Anything on the page!

Caroline It is on the page. Wig-wam.

Tim How does that describe the company?

Brian Maybe we are fighting the cowboys.

Tim Very good.

Angela *(crossing to Caroline.)* Where?

Caroline There. *(Pointing.)* Wig-wam.

Angela Win-win. It says win-win.

Caroline Well, I haven't got my glasses.

Angela Well, it might have been an idea for you to have brought them. You might have expected that there would be a bit of reading to do

Caroline Are you having a go? Don't you dare have a go at me.

Angela No I ...

Caroline Days, I've been back. Days. Three months it took me to get myself right. I shouldn't have come back. We could have managed without my wages, I'm sure we could, but he said the MOT is up on the car and it needs a new exhaust and how my money makes all the difference so I came in, and HR said they'd ease me back in gently and send me on a few training courses but it's too early. I knew it was. I can't deal with it. I shouldn't have come. *(She exits.)*

Brian Oh dear.

Angela What did I say?

Jacquie I told you that she had just come back from an extended break. You shouldn't pressure her.

Angela I didn't.

Tim By extended break, I take you mean that she's been on long term sick.

Jacquie Yes.

Angela With stress?

Jacquie She called a customer a trumped-up, self-opinionated, sadistic, overblown excuse for a moron.

Angela Ah.

Jacquie With a tiny little willy.

Tim She was customer facing, then?

Jacquie Worked her way up, apparently.

Brian I remember her. She used to work in IT. She was on the helpdesk.

Tim And being in the call centre listening to disgruntled holiday makers is a promotion?

Brian I was that or the sack I think. She was totally useless.

Tim How hard can it be to tell someone to reboot their computer?

Jacquie I was thinking of working on the helpdesk.

Brian You?

Jacquie Why not?

Brian Well, I suppose if they employed Caroline...

Jacquie What are you trying to say?

Brian What are your skills in that area?

Jacquie I've got a computer at home.

Brian Ooh. Pardon me, Bill Gates.

Angela Brian, this is a company that allows its staff to flourish. If a fish was judged purely on its ability to ride a bicycle it would have a very low opinion of itself.

Brian What?

Tim I didn't know fish had opinions of themselves.

Angela The key is to find that talent and let it go!

Tim Hello and welcome to Britain's Coastal Water's Got Talent. What's your name and where do you come from?

Brian I'm Harry the Haddock and I'm from near Fleetwood.

Tim And what do you do near Fleetwood, Harry?

Brian I'm a plasterer but I always wanted to be...

Tim Yes?

Brian To be...

Tim Yes?

Brian A Ventriloquist!

Tim No!

Brian Yes!

(Tim now becomes Brian's dummy.)

Tim Gottle a geer. Gottle a geer.

Brian Introduce yourself to the nice ladies.

Tim Hello. I'm Threddy the thith.

Brian Threddy the thith?

Tim Yeth.

Brian Freddy the fish?

Tim Thath what I thaid.

Brian Have you got a lisp?

Tim No, but itth dithicult to thay theth and thetheth without moving your lipth.

Brian Bit unfortunate being called Freddy then, isn't it.

Tim My parentth were arthholeth.

Brian Language, Timothy!

Tim They didn't even thend me to thcool.

Angela I thought all fish went to school, ha ha.

Tim Ith thith audienth partithipathion?

Brian So you were traumatised in childhood?

Tim Yeth. Thatth why I thuck thumbth.

Angela Fish don't have thumbs.

Tim I thuck other peopleth. I thuppothe a thuckth out of the quethtion.

(Brian and Tim high five as though they have achieved their objective.)

Angela Well that was very amusing, and a nice little ice breaker. It's a shame Caroline missed it.

Tim I'm not thucking her!

Angela Yes, no. Thank you Tim. But it would be nice if we could demonstrate a bit of compassion.

Jacquie I've been nice to her.

Angela You have. Thank you Jacquie. Now, let us bear that in mind what she has been through for the rest of the session. If she comes back, we should take this as an opportunity to help ease her back into work.

Brian You can rely on us.

Tim Absolutely.

Angela *(Unconvinced.)* Good. Remember what I said at the beginning. We trust each other here, and I can add that we also support each other. I hope that we can establish a relationship here today that will last long after the session is over.

Tim *(Mock shock.)* Angela! I'm a married man.

Angela A working relationship Tim. *(She stares at him for an uncomfortably long time. Caroline comes back.)* Ah! Caroline. Had a bit of a freshen up? *(Caroline scowls at her.)* Good. OK, moving on. Um. Where were we?

Tim Fish without bicycles.

Brian Or thumbs.

Angela Before that.

Brian Buzzword Bingo.

Tim Here's a phrase that sums up the company. Paperless Cubicle.

Brian That's true: there's never any in the gents.

Angela Where does it say that?

Tim   *(showing her)* There and there.

Angela   You're not supposed to combine the phrases! Oh never mind, we might as move onto the next thing on the agenda. Um. *(She looks at her notes.)* Oh, time for an ice breaker.

Brian   Yippee!

Tim   I thought we'd just had one.

Angela   Yes, and it was great fun but we need to do something that involves everyone.

Brian   You're the boss.

Angela   No, Brian. I'm just a facilitator. But if you work with me you might find that you get some benefit.

Tim   Really?

Angela   Yes, Tim. Really. I like to be as easy going as possible, but this is work time, you are on work premises and we are here we a purpose. Capisce?

Tim   *(surprised by the sudden authoritative tone.)* Um. Yeah.

Angela   Now, I am sure that we have all played ABC, where we go round the room each of us saying a word that starts with the next letter of the alphabet. We are going to play that, but with a twist. I want you to be thinking about our purpose here today and choose words that might form part of the company mission statement. Sounds fun doesn't it?

Tim   Thrilling!

Angela   OK. I'll start. Absolute.

Tim   Bollocks!

Angela   Tim!

Tim   It starts with B.

Angela   If you can't behave I will…

Tim   Send me to the headmaster with a note? *(This is a courageous attempt at boldness from Tim which earns him an icy glare from Angela.)*

Angela   We'll start again, shall we? And can we all please try to make a constructive contribution. Now then. Attain.

Tim   Battered. *(He's a brave lad.)*

Brian   Cod.

               (Angela frowns at the boys.)

Jacquie   Digital.

Caroline   Environmentally friendly.

Tim   That's two words.

Angela   It doesn't matter. How about *(She wiggles her hips.)* funky.

Tim   George.

Brian   Harrison.

(Angela is about to speak but is cut off by Jacquie.)

Jacquie   Intelligent.

Caroline   Jewish.

(The boys guffaw.)

Angela   We are looking for a company mission statement here, Caroline.

Caroline   And? The owners are Jewish.

Angela   Yes, but we are looking for positive words.

Tim   Whoa, are you saying being Jewish is negative Angela?

Angela   No I…

Tim   Because if you are, you should know that there are laws against that sort of thing.

Angela   Of course I am not saying that there is anything wrong with being Jewish. I am just saying that it is not really a word you would expect to see in a mission statement.

Jacquie   And 'battered cod' and 'George Harrison' are?

Angela   Yes, I was going to say something about that as well. I'm glad to see you thinking outside of the box, but please try to keep the word relevant. OK everyone? We're doing really well, but let's have some modern happening words. I'll start us off again; *(With emphasis.)* Kinky!

Tim   Little.

Brian   Madam.

(The boys leer at Angela who again makes Tim uncomfortable with a stare. There is tension in the air until Jacquie speaks.)

Jacquie   Nationwide.

Caroline   Open.

Angela   *(looking directly at Tim, who doesn't notice because he is whispering something to Brian.)* Passionate.

Tim   *(imitating Brian Sewell.)* Quintessentially.

Brian   Renaissancesque.

Jacquie   Safe.

Caroline   Targeted.

Angela   Uber.

Tim   Volks.

Brian   Wagon.

Jacquie   Extraordinary.

(Tim is about to protest, but Angela fixes him with a glare that would freeze the ocean.)

Caroline   Youthful.

Angela   And zany. Good. Well, that has got the old grey cells working.

Caroline   Why are you two making a big joke of the whole thing.

Tim   We're just having a bit of fun.

Caroline   But it isn't fun, It's just annoying.

Tim   You might enjoy it if you loosened up a bit.

Angela   *(warning)* Tim.

Caroline   And what if I don't want to loosen up?

Tim   Then you'll always highly strung, I guess.

Caroline   Is that supposed to be a joke?

Tim   Caroline, I know why you've been off work, we all do, but I don't think it helps you if we pussyfoot around trying not to upset you.

Caroline   No one is asking you to.

Tim   Good.

Angela   Would it help to talk about it, Caroline?

Brian   Oh, God.

Caroline   It?

Angela   The reasons why you had to take time off work.

Caroline   That's no secret. I told a customer that he was being too demanding.

Tim   And that he had a tiny penis.

Angela   But what led you to tell him that?

Caroline   He was being a knob.

Tim   There you go, Angela. Does that answer your question? Can we move on?

Angela   So how about now? If you took that call now, do you think you would react in the same way?

Caroline   If he was being a knob.

Brian   The wonders of cognitive therapy.

Jacquie   I think a lot of it has to do with diet.

Tim   Ey?

Jacquie Too much meat in the diet. That's what causes aggression.

Tim   Who's aggressive?

Angela   Well, I've been a vegetarian most of my life.

Tim   Figures.

Jacquie What do you mean?

Tim   Well, she's the type isn't she. Veggies are all the same. Lonely, hang around libraries, watch black and white movies. Burn candles when they are having a bath.

Angela   What makes you think I'm lonely?

Jacquie Don't you think you're generalising a bit there, Tim?

Tim   I'm just saying. It's a lifestyle choice, and people who choose that lifestyle tend to be a certain type.

Angela   I'm not lonely.

Tim   I mean, you know Brian's not a veggie don't you. You don't have to ask.

Angela   I have a very fulfilling life.

Tim   And I'm willing to put money on you being a carnivore.

Caroline My brother-in-law is a vegetarian and he's a brick layer.

Brian   What?

Caroline I'm just saying.

Brian   Thank you for that.

Caroline He doesn't burn candles when he is having a bath.

Tim   How do you know?

Caroline He isn't the type.

Tim   Been sharing a bath with your brother-in-law have you Caroline? Now this is getting interesting.

Jacquie Come to think of it, Stan on security is a vegetarian. And he's built like a brick, um, side of a house.

Tim   Did he ask you to soap his back?

Angela   Well, we do seem to have gone a little of topic, so...

Caroline I did not have a bath with my brother-in-law. It was just a misunderstanding.

Brian   Ey?

Jacquie What was a misunderstanding?

Caroline When he was staying with us, when he had broken up with Susan, I didn't know he was in there...

Tim   Aye, aye.

Caroline I mean, there is no lock on the door. No point when it is just the two of us. So, I went in to have a shower and...

Angela You don't need to tell us this, Caroline.

Tim   Don't stop her now.

Caroline To be honest, I thought he must have gone to work, the house was so quiet. Otherwise I wouldn't have been walking around naked.

Brian   Oh God. Please take the image away!

Caroline And anyway it was over in a flash...

Tim   Flash being the operative word.

Caroline So I shouldn't really have got worked up about it, but it was the shock of seeing his big hairy...

Tim   Vegetarian sausage.

Caroline ...chest first thing in the morning, that it got me in a bit of a tizz. The rest of the day was a bit of a haze, so when that idiot started going on about his apartment not looking like the one in the brochure.

Tim   Oh. This happened the day you got...

Angela Advised to take a rest.

Caroline I just cracked.

Brian   So that's why willies were on your mind.

Angela Well, Caroline. I think it is very brave of you to share that story with us.

Caroline Oh well. I don't really know why I...

Angela Round of applause for Caroline everyone.

Tim   Do we have to?

Angela Come on. *(Leads the others in an unenthusiastic round of applause.)*

Angela Great. A little off topic but very useful.

Brian   Very!

Angela Now, if we can just think back a bit.

Tim   Only if we detour around that image of Caroline being naked.

Brian   Oh no. There it is again.

Angela The ABC game was all about words that some up this company. And that is what a mission statement is. A short sentence that says it all.

Brian   Can I ask something?

Angela   Yes Brian.

Brian   What is the point of all this? This is a big, national company. Why would they pick us four to come up with a new mission statement?

Angela   They wanted it to come from within. The opportunity to participate was open to all.

Brian   But the room is only set up for four. You knew it was only going to be us. We are hardly the crème de la crème are we? Me and Tim are only here for a skive; Caroline is *(carefully)* returning to work; and as for Miss Laminated Sign here!

Jacquie   What did you just call me?

Brian   It is you isn't it, that makes all them signs. 'Please return the milk to the fridge'. 'Please wipe up any spills'. 'Please think of others before adjusting the heating'. 'Will Gentlemen refrain from putting chewing gum in the urinals'? 'Please put paper towels in the bin provided'. 'Please ensure the bowl is clear before leaving the cubicle'.

Jacquie   The state of the men's toilets is disgusting.

Brian   Yes, but the laminated signs just make it worse. Do you think someone is going to drop the chewing gum into the urinal, see the sign and then fish it out again?

Jacquie   If men knew how to behave there would be no need for the signs.

Brian   There is no need for them anyway. I don't know, give someone a PC, a printer and a laminator and they turn into Big Brother. Don't do this, don't do that. Do you follow people round with you little laminating pouches?

Jacquie   Have you got a better idea. Perhaps we should let this place go to ruin.

Brian   Better that than having signs telling you when you can breathe!

Angela   Er yes, I think we have got a little off track again here.

Brian   Here's a mission statement for you. We don't imitate. We laminate!

Jacquie   If you are just going to sit there and take the piss, why don't do us all a favour and piss off?

Brian   I can't do that. I want to make a 'worthwhile contribution to the debate'.

Angela   If you could just turn the page in your booklet...

Jacquie   The last time you did something worthwhile your mummy had to change your nappy.

Brian   And you get a lot of job satisfaction, do you, sitting there behind your laminated counter?

Jacquie I have a very important role. I don't sit there browsing the internet all day like some. My job is all about health and safety and it doesn't get more important than that.

Brian   Health and Safety! You?

Jacquie I have to make sure people are behaving in a safe and responsible manner.

Brian   Oh, by spying on them on the CCTV you mean.

Jacquie And taking appropriate action if anyone is contravening guidelines.

Brian   By putting up a sign you mean. That's all you do isn't it? You see someone being naughty so you wait until they've gone and then creep up and put up a sign warning them not to do it again.

Jacquie It is an important deterrent.

Brian   It's not a deterrent. "There'll be no uncovered bowls in the microwave." What does it even mean?

Jacquie It's obvious what it means.

Brian   Yeah. That's why someone scribbled underneath "You're wrong. There's one in there now".

Jacquie And don't think I don't know who wrote that.

Brian   Well, it wasn't me, if that is what you are suggesting.

Jacquie Are you sure? Don't forget there is a camera in the kitchen. It would be easy enough for me to get hold of the tapes.

Brian   Oh yeah. And that would be a useful use of company resources wouldn't it. The countries down the pan, nobody wants to go on package holidays any more so the firm's on its last legs but at least we will know who is responsible for defacing your precious signs.

Angela   *(screaming.)* SHUT UP! *(There is a stunned silence.)* Right, you bunch of misfits, this stops here and it stops now. You might not be la crème de la crème. More like a lump of mouldy cheese stuck at the back of the fridge, but you are all I've got and I'm going to get a bloody mission statement out of you if it kills us all. *(Caroline starts to leave.)* Sit down!

Caroline I need to…

Angela   I said SIT! *(She does.)* Now, I want you to *(Spoken like a threat.)* turn the page in your booklet. *(They do.)* What does it say?

Tim   *(quietly)* Naughty but nice.

Angela   SPEAK UP.

Tim   *(normal voice)* Naughty but nice.

Angela   That's right. Naughty but nice. *(Coming from Angela it sounds like the most awful words ever spoken.)* What does it say under that?

Tim   Never...

Angela   Brian?

Brian   Um. Never knowingly undersold.

Angela   Yes. Never knowingly undersold. Caroline. What is the difference between 'naughty but nice' and 'never knowingly undersold'?

Caroline Er...

Angela   Yes.

Caroline One is about cakes?

(Angela takes off her suit jacket, throws it aside then loosens her blouse in preparation for the hard slog she anticipates. She crosses to the flipchart and writes 'Mission Statement' at the top of the page and 'Catch Phrase' half way down.)

Angela   Where does 'naughty but nice' go?

Jacquie Under...

Angela   Caroline?

Caroline Under 'Catch Phrase'.

Angela   Yes! That's right. *(She crosses to Caroline, stands behind her and puts her hands on her shoulders. Caroline is mortified.)* 'Naughty but nice' is a catch phrase. Now, Tim. *(She crosses to Tim and presses her bosom into Tim's terrified face before lowering her own face so that it is an inch from his. When she speaks it is full of menace.)* Where does 'never knowingly undersold' go?

Tim   M, m, m, mission statement.

Angela   Yes Tim. Never knowingly undersold is a mission statement. *(She crosses to the flipchart and writes 'naughty but nice' under catch phrase and 'never knowingly undersold' under mission statement.)* So, now we have made some progress. We know the difference between a catch phrase and a mission statement, don't we? *(Silence.)* DON'T WE? *(Everyone quickly agrees.)* Good. *(She winks at a traumatised Tim.)* So what is it? *(Silence.)* WELL?

Brian   *(hesitatingly)* A mission statement says something about the company.

Angela   Like 'Jewish'?

Brian   Something about the purpose of the company.

Angela   Something about the purpose of the company. Very good Brian. I knew you could do it. So now that we know what a mission statement is, perhaps we can make one up. Eh? What do you think Jacquie with a Q?

Jacquie   *(quickly)* Yes. Certainly.

Angela   Good. So what is the purpose of this company?

Brian   We, um. We sell package holidays.

Angela   Yes Brian, we sell package holidays. But what is our purpose?

Brian   To er, send people on holiday.

Angela   Is that it? So long as they actually go on holiday have we achieved our goal?

Brian   Um, well…

Angela   Do we not want them to have the best damn holiday in history?

Brian   Well. Yes. I suppose so.

Angela   So all you have to do is think up a sentence that says that, ok? *(With menace.)* OK? *(Everyone quickly agrees.)* Good. *(Angela re-arranges her blouse, retrieves her jacket and puts it back on. Pats her hair, composes herself then smiles the sweetest of smiles to the group. She crosses to the flipchart and turns the page over. She turns and smiles at the group.)* Time for a brainstorm. Words for a mission statement. Everyone knows how a brainstorm works, yes? Just say whatever comes into your head.

Caroline   Um…

Angela   Yes dear?

Caroline   Happy.

Angela   Very good! Happy. *(She writes it on the flipchart, as she does other words and phrases suggested during the following)*

Jacquie   Sunny.

Caroline   Clean.

Tim   Sand.

Brian   Sea.

Tim   Warm sea.

Brian   Golden Sand.

Angela Yes.
Caroline Excursions.
Jacquie Local Flavours.
Caroline Relaxing.
Jacquie Fun.
Brian Satisfied customers.
Angela Good.
Caroline Value for money.
Brian Beaches.
Caroline Hotels.
Brian Restaurants.
Jacquie Entertainment.
Angela Some more.
Caroline Chartered flights.
Brian Family friendly.
Jacquie Safe.
Caroline Great holidays.
Jacquie Karaoke.
Angela Excellent. I think we have all we need now. Don't you think so? An excellent selection of words and it is there isn't it? Doesn't it just leap out at you? Look. *(She circles the words as she reads them out.)* Happy, customers, Happy, *(again.)* holidays. Happy Customers, Happy Holidays. Isn't that just a great mission statement? *(General murmuring. Everyone is just glad it is over.)* It just goes to show what teamwork can achieve. We have done exactly what we set out to do. *(She turns a page of the flipchart to reveal a fresh page which has* **New Company Mission Statement Happy Customers, Happy Holidays** *already neatly printed on the page.)*
Tim *(astonished)* It had already been decided?
Angela No Tim. *(She crosses to him and gently strokes his cheek.)* We came up with it. This team. That's what the next company newsletter will say and that is what you will tell anyone who asks. *(Menacingly)* Isn't it? *(Everyone agrees.)* Good. Well, as we have worked so well together it means that we have finished a little early I suggest that we fetch the lunch and then we can all get back to our desks this afternoon. *(Moving toward the exit.)* Come on Tim.
Tim Me?

Angela   Yes, you can help me carry the tray.
         (Tim is reluctant but joins her. Angela is triumphant.)
         End

More Plays by David Muncaster
Community Spirit
Full Length Farce - 8m 3f
The village of Snickerton has a new community hall and all the local groups get together to organise an opening day that will never be forgotten. Pity Mel, the poor official from the local council who has to try to keep apart the warring factions.

There is Mike, the bombastic chairman from the choral society, who clashes with Chris, his deadly rival, as well as just about anyone else who dare to disagree with him. Add a couple of luvies from the am dram, some representatives of Churches Together who couldn't be further apart, the leader of the cubs and beavers who sees things in the night, and a host of other characters including a caretaker with a very unfortunate name.

Community Spirit is a large cast play with eleven speaking roles and any number of none speaking roles that starts out as a comedy of manners but by the end is pure farce.

Great fun for any theatre group looking to involve as many of their members as possible.

Mad Gary's Fruit and Nut Case
Full Length Comedy Thriller - 4m 4f
It is a big day for Tommy. His lovely daughter Peaches has just married Lionel Looselips, the son of the biggest fruit and veg wholesale magnate in the whole of the county. Now Tommy can be assured that his market stall will always have the freshest, best value produce known to man. The wedding reception is a grand affair, friends and relations are joined by rivals who, for one day, put their differences aside; or do they? As the ceremonial fruit salad is consumed the guests start dropping like fruit flies.

Who is responsible for this murderous act? What did they hope to gain? Who will be next? It's a job for "Mad" Gary Grasslover of the local constabulary. This intentionally corny and ribald comedy/murder mystery provides plenty of laughs and opportunity for the audience to join in the fun by, not only trying to guess the murderer, but also by selected members being given characters to play.

Waiting for a Train

Full Length Play - 4f

Set on the platform of a rural railway station waiting for a train that never comes, this is a play about life, love and hope. The stark reality of living with schizophrenia is contrasted by the warmth and playfulness that exists between the main characters. With a degree of flexibility in casting and a set that would work better if it is suggested rather than detailed this is play should be relatively simple to stage at the same time giving the actors the opportunity to immerse themselves into characters that have great complexity and depth.

Fresh Showers for the Thirsting Flowers

One Act Play - 2f

Alice is a retired English teacher who is living a comfortable if rather lonely existence. A chance encounter with her neighbour's daughter re-awakens her passion to teach when she discovers that most unusual of things. A pupil who wants to learn! With a respectful nod to 'Educating Rita' this is a story of how a generation gap is easily bridged through the discovery of a mutual interest. All scenes are set in Alice`s living room which has minimal set requirements. The title of this play is taken from the poem 'The Cloud' by Percy Bysshe Shelley. Other quotes in this play are considered 'fair usage' and do not contravene copyright law but a licence is required to use the music specified.

Mission Impossible

One Act Play - 2m 3f

A meeting room, a flip chart, an enthusiastic facilitator, and four employees who are determined to give her a hard time. This is the background to Mission Impossible, a hilarious look at the corporate nonsense that anyone who has ever attended a team bonding session will know only too well. Ice Breakers and silly games do little to bond this team as the beleaguered facilitator gets tough to ensure that she gets the outcome she desires. Mission Impossible won the Congleton One Act Play Festival 2009. This is an extended version of the original play and is a little bit longer, a little bit ruder and quite a bit sillier.

www.ingramcontent.com/pod-product-compliance
Lightning Source LLC
Chambersburg PA
CBHW060608030426
42337CB00019B/3660